Varina Anne Davis

An Irish knight of the 19th century

Sketch of the life of Robert Emmet

Varina Anne Davis

An Irish knight of the 19th century
Sketch of the life of Robert Emmet

ISBN/EAN: 9783337125042

Printed in Europe, USA, Canada, Australia, Japan

Cover: Foto ©ninafisch / pixelio.de

More available books at **www.hansebooks.com**

AN IRISH KNIGHT

OF THE

19TH CENTURY

Sketch of the Life of Robert Emmet

BY

VARINA ANNE DAVIS

NEW YORK
JOHN W. LOVELL COMPANY
14 AND 16 VESEY STREET

TROW'S
PRINTING AND BOOKBINDING COMPANY,
NEW YORK.

PUBLISHER'S NOTE.

"An Irish Knight" tells the fine and simple story of Robert Emmet; but, as his story was also the history of Ireland for the space of his short life, the writer—Miss Davis, the daughter of Jefferson Davis, whose recent visit to the North will be remembered—deals in "An Irish Knight" not only with the adventurous and romantic life, and tragic death of the patriot, but with the conditions which created the need for such a man, and with the sad tale of Ireland, in which he became so nobly but so fatally implicated.

AN IRISH KNIGHT.

Every man, be he never so great a genius, is to some extent the creature of his century. Shakespeare wrote of Hamlet's father's ghost with a sincerity and reverence which astonishes his modern readers; Goethe believed in the divine right of kings, and Gibbon, affected by the prevalent atheism of Young France, speaks but slightingly of the birth and progress of Christianity. If this be true of literature, where men have either to do with records of past events or with the creations of their own imaginations, how much more so is it with a politician or patriot, whose chances of success depend solely upon his ability to crystallize the ever-varying temper of the masses and make the populace, that "many-headed monster thing," serve to attain his ends.

Therefore, it seems necessary to take a cursory glance at Irish politics anterior to the time of Robert Emmet, before it will be possible to understand the motive power which could force a man possessed of birth and fortune into the arms of rebellion and treason.

Before the Danish invasion, toward the end of the eighth century, under Fergus, Ireland seems, from the beautiful account left us by the "Four Masters," to have realized the ideal of a "land flowing with milk and honey;" blessed in the humane Brehon law; blessed in the possession of a country eminently adapted to the grazing of their herds, their chief wealth, and lastly, blessed in the possession of the Christian faith. From her had emanated the first rays that had penetrated the heathen darkness of Germany, Helvetia, and England. Her monasteries were so renowned for their learning that students came from the main continent of Europe to sit at the feet of Irish teachers, and although *agriculture* was in its infancy, the wonderful tombs of the kings, and those round towers that crown many of the heights (the despair of archæologists), prove that they were well acquainted with the laws of architecture.

Such was the condition of Ireland when first invaded. What was her status when Henry II., in 1171, made use of a Bull granted by Adrian IV. ceding "the territory of Ireland" to him?

Torn by internal dissensions, united only, like clouds, by the storm-blast of foreign invasion, to be parted again by the whirlwinds of self-interest, Ireland presents the mournful picture of a country which for nearly four centuries had been a prey to civil war. Learning, that child of gentle Peace, had taken to herself the wings of the morning and flown to the uttermost ends of the earth. However, the Brehon law still, in a measure, preserved humanity among the contending tribes, and the septal arrangement insured to every man his own tract of land, with a joint ownership in the tribal grazing ground.

This state of independent proprietorship was, however, to cease. Henry II. insisted on the introduction of the feudal law of tenure of lands, held directly from the Crown, a system totally foreign to either the spirit or letter of the tribal conditions under which the Irish had formerly existed, thereby laying the foundation of that land agitation which to this day forms the chief disturbing element in British politics.

The second great factor in the disaffection of the Irish people is the adverse legislation which, python-like, has since 1295 crushed, in its tortuous folds, the frame around which Ireland could alone hope to build a system of equal representation, namely, amalgamation. It was in vain that marriage with an Irishwoman was declared a penal offence, vain that they were subjected to the indignity of proclaiming their nationality by a black patch on the side of the face, vain also that a man could be executed and his lands confiscated, if he presumed to wear his hair long, or let his mustache grow, according to Irish custom. The attractions of the Irish maidens proved too strong for the prohibitory statutes, and intermarriages continued to take place. Fifteen years after Cromwell's invasion, the children of some of his troopers could not speak a word of English!

To kill an Irishman was considered no crime by any English court, and, as late as 1647, Irish women and boys were shipped as slaves to the West India Islands.

The third, and probably greatest, cause of Irish hatred of English supremacy, has been one which would awaken the sympathy of any lover of freedom; namely, religious persecution. The Roman Catholics, to which denomination the larger part of the native population belonged, were subjected, as were also the Presbyterians, to a tyranny rivalling any practised in the Netherlands. Prohibited from buying land, from holding a lease, and, lastly, from the free exercise of their religion, they were enjoined, on pain of death and forfeiture of their property, to leave their children uneducated; the privilege was also denied of sending them abroad to acquire that instruction which was refused at home by this truly paternal Government. To promote the better execution of this humane statute, a premium of one-third of his father's estate was offered to any son informing against his recusant parent. A wife, too, by joining the Episcopal Church, could obtain a large portion of her husband's income, together with the permission of the law to marry again without forfeiting her alimony.

No Catholic was allowed to possess a horse valued at more than five pounds, in which case any Protestant might tender him the Test-oath, and on his refusing to take it, seize both his steed and lands.

Marriages between persons of different creeds were declared unlawful, and the children of such unions illegitimate. These poor people, whose religion was their only crime, were debarred from entering the army, navy, or practising at the bar. The career of a politician was closed to them by the Test-oath, as were also the colleges, and if a Catholic ventured into trade, he was again met by the regulation that no recusant should have more than two apprentices. The crowning statute was passed in the reign of George II., by which every Roman Catholic was deprived of his vote.

Remembering this persecution, we can well understand how the people rose against the payment of tithes to support a clergy so intimately connected with the Government that it was naturally concluded religious persecution emanated from them. While their own ecclesiastics were driven from the country with a price set upon their heads, it is hardly to be expected that the Irish would bear in silence the imposition of a tax to support a Church of which they did not approve.

True, a few priests were allowed to remain, but stationed so far apart, and the laws so stringent against their overstepping the boundaries of their parishes, that they only served, like a feeble rush-light in the catacombs, to intensify the surrounding gloom. The clergy, too, of the established Church were, with rare exceptions, absentees, whose poorly paid curates had not the heart or the energy to persuade the people into their manner of thinking.

So the work of sowing the wind went merrily on; but the Irish, like their emblematic shamrock, only grew the more luxuriant for this trampling, and before 1660 Irish ships and Irish enterprise were beginning to be recognized as factors in the commerce of the world. The Liverpool merchants then immediately raised such a cry that the Government was persuaded into the very wise expedient of putting a quietus to Irish trade by providing, in the "Ship Bill" of 1660, that it should be illegal for any Irish vessel to enter the carrying trade; and later, that Ireland should only be allowed to export her goods to Milford, Chester, and Liverpool. Thus Stafford crushed out the enterprise which promised to make the " Green Isle " bloom again.

It has been said by some that England was bound to repress the tendency to rebellion by stringent statutes. That this argument is utterly false and pernicious will be evident to any thinking mind. When is a man most ripe for revolution—when he has a large fortune at stake, or when he has nothing to lose, and probably all to gain? It was not the bourgeoisie of Paris that led the Revolution, but the ragged denizens of the Faubourg St. Antoine. It was the armed peasants of the mountains, and not the titled gentlemen of Rome, who first raised the standard of United Italy. To come nearer home, the revolt which set America free was led, not by the great lords whose plantations were equal to a dukedom in extent and revenue, but by a man springing from plain people, and educated as a simple surveyor. No man can strike as good a blow when his heart is with his money-bags. Had the gentlemen of Ireland always stood true to the peasantry, the dissolution of the union had not now been the chief perplexing problem of English politics.

That such a penal code should have been followed by rebellions innumerable is not surprising; that the people should have been repressed with wanton cruelty was the sequel to be expected. Sir Walter Raleigh thought it a worthy deed to put a whole garrison to the sword without mercy, after their surrender, on condition that their lives should be spared. Lord Ormond boasted that he had put to death eighty-eight captains, fifteen hundred and forty-seven rebels, and four thousand others.

Famine and pestilence, those two gaunt sisters of war, followed close upon her footsteps, so that, in the time of Elizabeth, Froude tells us, "The lowing of a cow or the sound of a ploughboy's whistle was not to be heard from Valentia to the Rock of Cashel." Nor was this the *only* occasion on which whole towns were depopulated and counties laid waste. Cromwell's proceedings in Wexford and Drogheda are another instance of this kind; as well as the depopulation attendant upon the colonization system under James, Charles I. and II., William III., and George I.

During the ensuing period, the fire of Irish animosity was kept aglow by repeated acts of cruelty through which the Government sought to quell the rising tide of liberalism. However, in the year 1782 a free Irish Parliament was again established by the efforts of Grattan, supported by the volunteers, who, with arms in their hands, were in a position rather to demand than petition their rights. Their efforts were, as may be imagined, hailed with delight and gratitude by their oppressed fellow-countrymen, and had this body been allowed to exist for a longer period there is little doubt that Ireland would now be a land rich in commerce, rich in agriculture, and richest in peace; but the promises of England to this unhappy country have ever been like the gifts of fairies, which crumble into dust at the first touch of the morning sunshine. So, the freedom which Grattan's magnificent eloquence had reconquered for his people, was bought of a carefully packed parliament, in no sense representative of the country, for the sum of £1,260,000, twenty-two Irish, six English peerages, twenty-two promotions and forty-eight patents of nobility. Having cursorily reviewed the general march of Irish history down to the Union, which now hangs in such a delicate balance, we have reached the time of the illustrious, though unfortunate, subject of this sketch.

Robert Emmet was born March 4, 1782. He was the youngest son of that Robert Emmet who, for many years, filled the office of State Physician in Dublin. Dr. Emmet seems to have held most patriotic views as to the duties a man owed his country, and to have early impressed his children with these opinions. Curran tells us of the "morning draught" of freedom which he gave his sons. We catch a glimpse of him asking his eldest child, Temple, "What he would do for his country?" "Addis," the second, "would kill his sister for Ireland."

Temple, alas, did not, like his brothers, live to exemplify the deep root their father's precepts had taken. He was cut off in the full bloom of his promising manhood, not, however, before having made a name for himself at the Irish bar as a young fellow "who knew more law and divinity than any judge or bishop of them all."

Thomas Addis Emmet became an exile, and died in America, because of his efforts for equal representation, and the career of Robert is one long story of patriotic devotion.

Unlike Byron, no one seems to have had a premonition of his coming greatness, so the records of his childhood are but meagre. We hear, however, that he possessed remarkable aptitude for exact sciences, especially mathematics and chemistry, which, indeed, he continued to study until his death. He had an inveterate habit of biting his finger-nails, which at one time came very near abridging the record of his life to but small compass. When still a child, he had one day been experimenting with corrosive sublimate, but, taking up his algebra, became engrossed in a difficult problem, and fell into his usual habit of biting his nails; the consequence was an attack of severe pain caused by the poison. However, this peculiar little fellow consulted the Encyclopædia and finding chalk to be the antidote, took it and crept to bed without alarming anyone. " When he came down to breakfast next morning," says an eye-witness, " his face was as little and yellow as an orange, and he told a gentleman that he had suffered greatly during the night." Nevertheless, the algebraic problem was solved. Very strongly does the picture rise before us of this strange, knightly child, who met the probability of death with the same utter fearlessness which formed so marked a characteristic of his after life. How eagerly must this boy have drunk in the stories of oppression and tyranny of which Irish history is but the partial record! How must his young heart have answered to the call of liberty, that goddess who ever smiles fairest upon her most youthful devotees! How his bright eyes must have shone as he listened to the tales of generosity and daring that are associated with the names of O'Moore, Geraldine, and Sarsfield! It was at the feet of his father that Robert Emmet learned to love down-trodden Ireland better than his life.

He was sent to school at an early age and came, immediately previous to his entrance into the University, under the care of one Dr. Lewis, who, although a minister of the Episcopal Church, was a liberal man and fully awake to the injustice of Catholic disfranchisement.

In 1793, when fifteen years of age, Emmet became a member of Trinity College, Dublin, where his career was marked by brilliant success, both as a student and orator. Moore gives a picture of him at this time drawn with such a loving hand, that the young patriot seems to live again, clothed in all that ineffable sweetness and personal magnetism which made men and women in after years suffer torture and death rather than betray his hiding place.

What a gay life the collegiates of that day enjoyed! Their parties out to Dalkey, where they crowned a monarch with all the ceremonial of regal state; the pasquinades they wrote against the government, the songs they sung, and lastly, the suppers, in consequence of which the "king lost his crown while measuring both sides of the road on his way home," as Moore expresses it.

There is much doubt whether Emmet took part in any of these mummeries; to him, young, all aglow with the burning desire of freedom, and the ever poignant sorrow for his oppressed country gnawing at his heart, that men should waste their time on masquerades must have seemed worse than frivolous.

No one takes life so seriously as young people, that is, when seriousness does become a factor in their theory of existence. The old have reconciled themselves to much, relinquished many hopes, and even to the boldest democrat gray hairs seem to bring a modicum of conservatism. Many a weary man drops his oar as age comes upon him, and drifting with the stream of events, forgets in his selfish ease the Charybdis of anarchy and the Scylla of despotism which await the helpless ship of state.

Moore tells us that when he entered the University, Emmet was already celebrated for the wonderful purity of his life, as well as for the remarkable qualities of his genius.

These two, so unlike, yet having so

many points in common, seem to have drawn very close together. Emmet, who was passionately fond of music, would sit for hours listening to the melodies he loved played by "Little Tommy;" and one evening, when he struck the last chords of "Let Erin remember the day," Emmet sprang to his feet exclaiming, " Oh, were I at the head of twenty thousand men, marching to that tune——" Yet this high-souled young Irishman never mentioned the plans of that society to which he already belonged ; but when, during one of the long country walks they took together, he discovered that Moore was the author of a very revolutionary letter which appeared in "The Press," a liberal organ of that time, in his wonderfully sweet voice and with " a gentleness almost feminine," he persuaded the rash boy to hold himself aloof from the political movements of the day. He then went on to expound his theory of a man's true duty to his country—to act, not merely to write or speak. It is a singular instance of generosity on the part of Emmet, that he should not have sought to enlist the already budding genius of his friend in Ireland's cause, for which himself had ventured life and honor.

At this time the whole island was ablaze with patriotic agitation. The broken faith of the English crown, and the disappointed hopes of the persecuted Catholics, caused widespread dissatisfaction among the rank and file of the people, and cast many into the outstretched arms of the United Irishmen. The discovery of the proselyting efforts of this society gave rise to a timorous and unworthy policy on the part of the government. The pretext of outrages committed by the "Defenders," was the cause assigned for putting the coercion act into practice, by which any man being found out of his house between sundown and six in the morning, rendered himself liable to arrest, and if unable to give an account of his business satisfactory to the officer in command, was transported to an English man-of-war, where he was forced to serve as a sailor.

The militia, chiefly composed of Orangemen, were permitted to break into any house, at whatsoever hour they pleased, to search for arms, or to ascertain if anyone besides the regular occupants was within. That a party of men exasperated by constant outrages and reprisals should not have been the best preservers of the peace in a country already ripe for rebellion, can easily be imagined, and one is not surprised to learn that in every county under military law, the emissaries of " The United Irishmen" should have found fruitful soil, and that the branch societies should have grown with the rapidity of Jonah's gourd.

Pillage, murder, and arson are not the best methods of pacifying a gallant people, and well might the " Receipt to make a Rebel " have been given as follows:

"Take a loyal subject, uninfluenced by title, place, or pension, burn his house over his head, let the soldiery exercise every species of insult and barbarity toward his helpless family, and march away with the plunder of every part of his property they choose to save from the flames."

At such a period it could hardly be that the college of which Emmet and Tone were members should remain totally free from the prevailing temper of the times. The historical society, which had dragged out an intermittent existence since 1770, now became a powerful engine for disseminating patriotic and liberal views among the students. Here Emmet was destined to win fresh laurels by his eloquence; although toward the end of his residence in the University all references to modern history were strictly prohibited, he was able, by subtle allusions and apt parallels, to raise the enthusiasm of his fellows to fever heat.

Moore has preserved for us two of their subjects of discussion. "Is a democracy or aristocracy most favorable to the advancement of science and art, and whether a soldier is at all times bound to obey the order of his commanding officer." That Emmet was the glowing advocate of democracy and the liberty of a soldier to act according to his own conscience, is of course understood. Strange havoc this idea would have made among the serried legions of a Cæsar, or the rapidly wheeling columns of a Napoleon; and still greater among the heterogeneous mass, chosen from all nations, with which the great Frederick held the allied German powers in check.

Emmet was to see the day when he realized fully the necessity of strictest discipline in an army, and the dangers consequent upon every man judging for himself, while the general was held responsible for the conduct of all. "So exciting and powerful," says Moore, "were the speeches of Emmet, and so little were the most distinguished speakers among our opponents able to cope with his eloquence, that the Board, at length, actually thought it right to send among us a man of advanced standing in the University, and belonging to a former race of good speakers in the society, in order that he might answer the speeches of Emmet, and endeavor to obviate what they considered the mischievous impression produced by them."

Not many months after this event the storm broke, the plot was discovered, the French expedition under Hoche did not arrive. "The elements seemed," says Walpole, "to fight for England," and indeed, in this case adverse winds detained them on the French coast till the tide in the affairs of Ireland, which might have borne her on to independence, was at the ebb, and only served to throw her unhappy children upon the treacherous quicksands of English mercy.

Emmet's brother, Thomas Addis, was, in 1798, arrested and committed to Newgate prison, on the same day that the Executive Committee was seized at the house of Oliver Bond, where they were in session. This movement initiated the system by which the government proposed to crush the rebellion.

An examining board was created at the University, and the students were sworn on oath to divulge to the full extent their knowledge of the Society of United Irishmen, and to give the names of any person or persons whom they knew to be members. On receiving the news of this inquisition, Emmet wrote a letter to the board desiring his name to be withdrawn from the books of the college, which letter he first showed his father, and, having received his entire approval of the sentiments therein expressed, it was then forwarded. However, the dons took no notice of this communication, and he was enrolled among the expelled students.

Whatever the connection may have been between Emmet and the leaders of the United Irishmen, anterior to the discovery and frustration of their plans, it is an incontrovertible fact that he was well acquainted with their subsequent movements, and occasionally played the part of messenger for them during their imprisonment.

When Thomas Addis was removed to Fort George, in 1800, Emmet embraced the opportunity to leave the country, being, as he subsequently had reason to believe, already under government supervision. It was about this time that Dr. Emmet, overcome by the misfortunes of his eldest surviving son, sank into the grave, leaving Robert at that period of his existence when he most required the counsels of age to temper the untried ardor of his youth.

Emmet seems at first to have held aloof from the little colony of United Irishmen then seeking refuge in Paris, and to have travelled in Switzerland, Holland, and the French provinces; there is even a report, although not well authenticated, that under the assumed name of Captain Brown, he visited Cadiz.

After the banishment of the political prisoners, Emmet met his brother in

Amsterdam, from which city he posted direct to Paris, there to become one of that little coterie of disappointed patriots, and to infuse the ardent hopefulness of his own disposition into their desolate existence.

Thomas Addis soon followed him, and also joined this party who, relying upon the false promises of that great-little man Napoleon, were formulating the scheme of a second rising of " The United Irishmen." Bonaparte was, as ever, profuse in offers of assistance; yet even while negotiating with the two Emmets, and making, or at least pretending to make, preparations for a descent upon the Irish coast, Mr. Goldsmith tells us that the First Consul submitted proposals to the British Government, amounting virtually to a mutual extradition treaty. With the exception of the United Irishmen, no other recusant British subjects were in France; therefore, if we can accept Goldsmith's account, the perfidy of Bonaparte is truly appalling. There is, nevertheless, a certain alchemy in truth which makes it dangerous to use deception with a man of perfect integrity, and Robert Emmet possessed this quality to an extraordinary degree. In his interview with Napoleon, he seems with wonderful accuracy to have penetrated the motives of the First Consul, and to have determined just how far any reliance could be placed on the cooperation of French troops. " His," Bonaparte's, " only object was to aggrandize France and damage England, and, so far as that object went, to wish well to any effort in Ireland that might be ancillary to the purpose." Of

Talleyrand he held as unfavorable an opinion as of his master, although he believed the minister really did desire a republic to be established in Ireland, whereas Bonaparte's hope was her annexation to France, thereby closing England in a vice so powerful that her commerce and liberties would soon fall a prey to the Gallic army. This opinion being shared by his brother, the two Emmets became the heads of what was called the Anti-French party, among the exiles; that is to say, they only desired as much recognition from the Republic as she had vouchsafed the American colonies; while the other party proposed but to change masters, and for an Anglo-Saxon oppression substitute a Gallic tyranny.

It was about this time that the famous conspiracy under Major Despard rose so prominently upon the horizon of English politics. There is little doubt, from the accounts of the secret manipulations of the press, given us by Goldsmith, but that Despard had the countenance, if not the assistance of the French Government. Many indications point to the fact that he was not, as was generally believed at the time, an assassin, whose only object was to kill King George, but that, in reality, it was an English radical insurrection which was so anxiously looked for by the exiles in Paris.

During all these two years of comparative peace Emmet had been employing himself with the study of military science. There can be nothing more touching than the vision of this young knight preparing himself for "that weird battle in the West," where, like

Arthur, he was to fall fighting for his people. Amid all the gayety and beauty of the French capital, that Athens of our modern civilization, he seems to have lived a life apart, keeping his vigils over that armor of knowledge which he hoped to don in his day of trial. There are numerous books on tactics in existence which are interlined, annotated, and bracketed in his hand, with a care and discrimination only possible to a close student. He seems to have given particular attention to those portions bearing upon defensive warfare and the modes of encampment and attack in a mountainous country.

In the month of October, 1802, he was sent by his colleagues in Paris to investigate the proceedings of Major Despard's Irish agent Dowdall. However, as the treaty of March 27th had set the long rankling disputes of England and France at rest for a short time, there was but little hope of a successful rebellion.

Arrived in Ireland, Emmet conversed with several men of consequence, who advised him on no account to give up the proposed agitation of Irish liberty; proffering their ready assistance in funds and service. Be it here observed, that not one of those influential persons, whose names were carefully concealed, ever rendered any of that longed-for aid which had been so lavishly promised. Emmet said of them: "There were many who professed to serve a cause with life and fortune, but, if called upon to redeem their pledge, would contrive to do it with the lives and fortunes of others. For my part, my fortune is now committed, the promises of many whose fortunes were considerable are committed likewise, but their means have not been as yet forthcoming."

Until the following March, Emmet seems to have gone a good deal into general society, although closely watched by the Government. He took up his abode at a country-place belonging to his father, and there constructed a number of secret chambers and passages, on which he no doubt relied to find a safe asylum in time of danger.

The personal appearance and manner of Robert Emmet at this time, as it has been transmitted to us by those who knew and loved him, is about as follows: Slenderly made, he yet possessed great symmetry of frame and grace of motion, combined with almost inexhaustible powers of endurance; he was small in stature, being only five feet eight inches high; of a dark complexion, with black hair; his eyes were not large, but singularly expressive. His forehead was well shaped, the brow broad and high, his nose thin and straight; his manner in conversation was habitually quiet, but cheerful, never tinged by either the braggadocio that marks the coward or the recklessness of the typical Irishman. Moore says, in one of his letters, " My poor friend Emmet was as gentle as a girl." It was only when speaking on that subject which lay nearest his heart—the wrongs and sufferings of his beloved Ireland—that the whole man seemed to become transfigured. His wonderful voice, which, without apparent effort, could fill a crowded hall, or ring through the secluded dells where the society met, seemed to become the very spirit of the man and his whole body but the instrument on which it played.

It was about this period that he met Sarah, youngest daughter of the barrister John Curran. This beautiful and accomplished young woman had the good fortune to call forth as true and pure an affection as ever warmed a manly breast, and shared in future in Emmet's heart the throne his country had, until now, wholly usurped. That these two divinities could exist side by side in a soul as mighty as his is evinced by the utterances recorded for us by one of those who truly revered the noble qualities of this young patriot.

The night before the rebellion, when encouraging a fellow-conspirator with whose lady love Emmet was acquainted, he said: "The stagnant veil of inglorious ease is for those domestic, enamored souls who are content to pass their life in inactive worthlessness, and who wish to enjoy affection without having merited love. Mine is a higher ambition. I must make myself worthy of the woman of my choice. Heaven forbid that an excusable passion should thwart the design of my life, or cause me for an instant to neglect my country's good for the purpose of promoting my own personal advantage." Beneath the quaint and verbose style of the day is discernible that nobleness of principle which animated him through life. Well might he have exclaimed with Lovelace:

"I could not love thee, dear, so much,
Loved I not honor more."

It was in March of the year 1803 that Emmet commenced his first active preparations. The rupture of the

Treaty of Amiens and the proposed invasion of Great Britain, on the Irish coast, renewed the hopes of the patriots. Thomas Addis having had several audiences with Talleyrand and Bonaparte, and being now assured by them that "the Army of England" should leave the coast of Brittany in August, instructed his brother to begin operations for the collecting of arms and the organization of those counties where the cruelties of '98 still rankled in the remembrance of the people. They felt sure the standard of rebellion need only be raised to assemble an army large enough to form a considerable factor in the French chance of a successful invasion. Nor were these enthusiastic men alone in their opinion; from some letters taken on board the Admiral Alpin, and published in one of the

Parisian journals, we gather that all England dreaded the coming storm, and that Irish dissatisfaction was also a cause of great apprehension to many worthy gentlemen whose official position necessitated their being more or less acquainted with the real temper of the Government. Contemporaneous literature also is evidence that the constant fear of a descent upon the English coast, or the landing of a French army in Ireland, caused a panic, the like of which had not been witnessed since the Spanish Armada. It was, therefore, not such a visionary plan of Emmet's as has been generally supposed, or if so, he was, at least, kept in countenance by many brave and learned British subjects; and so Ireland, like Sisyphus, made one more effort to roll the stone of English supremacy up the steep hill of wealth and prejudice. Emmet's first step was to establish depots in different parts of Dublin for the manufacture and storage of munitions of war. In Patrick Street powder and rockets were made; in another house hollow beams were put together filled with combustibles, and the handles of those pointed pikes were constructed, on which Emmet placed so much reliance; he calls them, "the weapons of the brave." Of blunderbusses and pistols there seem to have been but few; probably on account of the difficulty in procuring funds. The depot in Marshalsea Lane was immediately under Emmet's own supervision, his chief officers being appointed to superintend the other manufactories. The workmen received no guerdon for their toil but food and lodging, sometimes only the latter; they labored exclusively for the love of Ireland and their leader, and although there were at least forty men in the employment of the society, it is most remarkable that the Government was obliged to introduce paid spies to discover their movements.

Emmet was now boarding with a Mrs. Palmer, of Harold's Cross, under the assumed name of Hewitt; but as the conspiracy took on grander proportions it was necessary for him to have a more secluded place of residence. He therefore took a house in Butterfield Lane, under the title of Robert Ellis, where he continued to reside, with several others of his party, until the 16th of June. The manner of life pursued by these daring young fellows has been preserved for us by Anne Devlin, the maid-of-all-work who attended them.

"They had," she says, " little or no furniture, and slept on mattresses laid upon the floor. They were always in good spirits, and Mr. Hamilton used often to sing; he was a very good singer; Mr. Robert used sometimes to hum a tune, though he was no great singer, he was the best and kindest-hearted of all the persons I ever knew. He was too good for many of those who were about him." She also entertained a high opinion of Russel, ranking him only second to "Mr. Robert."

It was here that Emmet harangued his fellow-conspirators, and from here that he made those excursions into the surrounding hill-country to meet the different bodies of United Irishmen, in lonely glens, where he confirmed the vacillating, as well as persuaded the opposed. One of the society has left us a vivid description of the dim starlight shining upon the open hillside, the silent figures disappearing down the valley, one by one, and the sudden apparition of armed men starting up out of the heather, as if by magic, when he reached the gorge's mouth. Once fairly inside, he was guided by the sweet tones of Emmet's voice, ringing through the darkness like a silver trumpet, and firing every heart with its call to arms. He remarks that the chief characteristic of Emmet's oratory was the evident genuineness of the sentiments he expressed, and the care he took to counsel moderation in victory, while he called upon the people to rise against oppression.

Malichy presented a singular instance of the reverse side of Irish character; his orations all tended toward exciting the worst passions of the peasantry. On this occasion, seeing a new face among the crowd, he suddenly cried, "A spy—a spy!" A circle of avoidance was immediately formed around the astonished intruder, but Emmet, perceiving his position, walked up and, taking his hand, said : "I am sure there must have been a mistake here. Mr. K—— is a young gentleman of liberal principles and high notions of honor. I am certain that he is incapable of betraying our secret, much less acting as a spy upon our proceedings." His confidence was not misplaced; K—— became one of his staunchest supporters.

The plan of the rebellion was greatly dependent upon the longed-for invasion of England; Emmet's hope was to seize the Castle at Dublin, the Pigeon House at the mouth of the river, Island Bridge, Cork Street and Mary Street Barracks, as well as the Customhouse; the coal quay also was to be held by the insurgents, as well as numerous houses all through the town which were to serve as batteries covering iron chains, stretched across the street in the manner of a barricade. These were to prevent the massing of regular troops in any one place.

Emmet himself was to have commanded the surprise of the Castle; this feat, which was rightly considered the key to a successful revolt, was very perfectly organized on paper. Emmet and about eighteen other daring spirits, were to enter the courtyard in coaches, as if on their way to a dinner-party. Being once within, they proposed to throw open the gates to the rebels, and at the same moment the insurgents were to swarm into the citadel from all sides, by means of scaling ladders suspended from the windows of the surrounding houses. The bridges were to be covered with boards pierced by strong iron spikes, to prevent cavalry charging over them on the insurgents. Large beams filled with combustibles were to be distributed in different parts of the town, to be set on fire if needed.

Dwyer, an outlaw of '98, whose story reads like one of Verne's wildest romances, was pledged to make a demonstration before the walls of the town in one direction, while another body were to distract the attention of the troops on the other side. In the meantime the arsenals and garrisons having been seized, Dublin would be in the hands of the United Irishmen. Emmet had in his different depots at the time the following munitions of war : 45 lbs. of cannon powder, 11 boxes of fine powder, 100 hand grenades, 62,000 rounds of musket-ball cartridges, 3 bushels of musket-balls, and a quantity of tow mixed with tar and other combustibles, as well as the beams before mentioned, skyrockets for signals, and 20,000 pikes.

He believed that his arrangements were a profound secret, but the subsequent disclosures of " Carotid-artery-cutting Castlereagh " prove that the Government was cognizant of them almost, if not quite, from the first.

The policy which allows men to rush blindly on to destruction, that their blood may prove a safe cement for the foundation of new tyrannies, is one which is abhorrent in the extreme to any right-minded person. That this has been the usual mode of dealing with Irish rebellions since the time of Elizabeth, is also an evident fact to those who read, with unprejudiced eyes, the history of Hibernian insurrections.

Buoyed up by the hope of success, and undismayed by the prospect of defeat, the conspirators drifted gayly on through the early summer. The time of the outbreak was fixed for August, when Napoleon was expected to provide ample work for the English soldiery on their own soil; but Fortune, who seemed from the first to frown upon the attempt of Emmet, here also intervened to force them to an earlier issue.

The first general alarm that the citizens received was on July 14th, when, in honor of the birth of a French republic, bonfires were lighted in different parts of Dublin, and the most decided hostility expressed toward the English government. This alone would not have served to arouse the vigilance of the authorities, had not an explosion taken place in the depot at Patrick Street on the 16th, caused by the drunken carelessness of a workman, which disclosed the existence of the depots. The munitions of war were, however, so speedily removed that the officer commissioned to search the premises, found nothing more suspicious than the apparatus for making gunpowder; but, unfortunately, in the hurry of departure a bag of flints had been dropped, which were picked up in the street and taken to the Castle, thereby affording conclusive evidence of military preparations being in progress.

Emmet had then, for the first time, to meet the demon of dissension. His staff, alarmed at the idea of premature movement, which now became the only chance of gaining their object, wished to draw back entirely ; he, however, refused to listen to the proposition, and partly by his eloquence, partly by the force of his personality, overcame their objections, and the day was fixed for July 23d.

From the time of the explosion, Emmet took up his abode in the Marshalsea depot, where, surrounded by the implements of warfare, he wrote proclamation after proclamation, and formulated a system of provisional government for the interregnum following the revolution. His indefatigable energy was now displayed to the greatest advantage. Inspecting the works, encouraging his assistants, attending to the printing of his proclamations, and holding constant councils with Dwyer and other partisan leaders, his time was entirely absorbed by the cause to which he truly said he had "sacrificed his life, his fortune, and his love."

In the afternoon of the 23d the Government received certain intelligence of the rising contemplated for that evening. Emmet had, in the forenoon, despatched an emissary to bring the coaches to Marshalsea Lane, in which he hoped to make an entrance into the castle; but the messenger, having embroiled himself in a fight between a soldier and a countryman, shot and killed Cornet Brown, and was obliged to fly, leaving the coachmen without orders. Emmet at this time was anxiously expecting their arrival. Confusion reigned supreme—dissensions in the councils and disorder in the depot. Since daylight there had been a constant influx of undisciplined countrymen. Anarchy was the spirit of the day. The insurgents sat in the tavern of John Rouke, singing and drinking; others filled the depot demanding weapons. "I was astonished," says an eye-witness, "at the fortitude of Emmet and Malichy, who continued to give orders and distribute arms." So great was the confusion that the quick and slow fuses became mixed. The flints were mislaid, and, owing to the density of the crowd, could not be found. The leaders, who should have been with their men, were carousing at the house of John Heavy, where, with but few exceptions, they remained even after the firing commenced.

Emmet was awaiting the appearance of the Kildare men, on whom he chiefly relied to surprise the different arsenals; but these brave patriots, most of whom had been "out" in '98, were met by some traitor, and told that the rebellion had been postponed, so they returned home, and with them went the hopes of Ireland.

Dwyer got no news of the change of date, as the messenger who was to have taken the intelligence did not leave the city. The Wicklow men massed in Dublin to great numbers; but, receiving no orders, and not seeing the signal rocket, returned the way they came.

While things were in this state, and the faculties of every man were strained to catch the approach of friend or foe, Quigley ran wildly into the depot exclaiming, "We are lost! the army is coming!" "Then," said Emmet, "it is better to die fighting than cooped up here." Seizing his sword he rushed into the street, followed by about eighty men. Although the alarm was false, when once fairly embarked upon the tide of revolution all retreat was cut off; they marched on, therefore, toward the castle, headed by their gallant leader. What was his horror when he heard that his followers, blinded by drink and excitement, had set upon and murdered Lord Kilwarden and his nephew, Dr. Wolf, who were passing in a coach. As soon as was practicable he made his way to the spot, and found that truly good man weltering in his blood, his half-distracted daughter standing beside him. Be it here noticed that Miss Kilwarden received no insult or injury from an Irish mob, even when they were infuriated by blood and liquor. Emmet took the poor girl by the hand, and led her to a place of safety, then returned to his men; but this momentary check to the impetuous movement of the insurgents destroyed the last chance of a successful revolution. Finding that he was no longer able to restrain his men, and that from the general of a patriot army, marching with high hopes to victory, he had degenerated into the leader of a riotous mob, he was about to retire. Not so Malichy. "Fire the signal," said he to the man who held the rocket; but Emmet insisted on longer delay. "Let no more blood be shed than is necessary," was his reiterated command. Just at that moment the troops came charging down upon them, and Emmet, crushing the fuse under his heel, gave the word to disperse. The military commenced firing, and the insurgents fled in all directions, some seeking refuge on the housetops, where they lay concealed behind chimneys and in gutters, and others again down the dark streets and narrow alleys.

So ended the Rebellion of July, born of a patriot's brain, nursed in a patriot's heart, and baptized in patriot blood.

On the night of the 23d Anne Devlin was aroused by knocking at the house in Butterfield Lane. On calling out to know who was at the door, Emmet answered her. " Oh! bad welcome to you. Is the world lost by you; cowards that you are, to lead the people to destruction and then leave them," she cried. " Do not blame me, the fault is not mine," said Emmet. She tells us that none of them ever upbraided Quigley, although this unhappy man was the real cause of their difficulties.

Emmet and his staff slept in Butterfield Lane that night; but early on Sunday morning they went to the house of Anne's father, where they would certainly have been taken had not the butler of Mr. Grierson sent word to Devlin to get them off as soon as possible, as their retreat had been discovered. He procured horses for three of them, and under his guidance they all escaped into the mountains, there to meet again, at the last council held with Dwyer, on the hillside. Not a moment too soon had they fled. Major Sirr with a party of yeomanry seized their first hiding-place. Finding it empty they demanded of Anne what she knew of the "Mr. Ellis" to whom it was leased. On her refusal to answer this question she was pricked with bayonets by these gallant militia-men until the poor girl lay bathed in her own blood, still remaining true to her master. She was then half hanged, but with a fortitude which should be honorably remembered by all Irishmen, she bore these tortures, as well as solitary confinement lasting two years, the imprisonment and ruin of her family, and insults innumerable, without revealing any of Emmet's secrets.

To return to the fugitives. Dwyer and the other leaders held a council, in which the voice of the majority was still for war; but here again the unselfish patriotism of Emmet was evinced. In vain did they persuade him that the whole country was ripe for revolt. He had seen but too plainly the hopelessness of the effort, and discountenanced all proposals that would necessitate renewal of bloodshed. " For," said he, " defeated in our first grand attempt all further endeavors must be futile. The justice of our cause must one day triumph ; let us not indiscreetly protract the period by any immature endeavors to accelerate it. No doubt I could, in forty-eight hours wrap the whole kingdom in the flames of rebellion ; but as I have no ambition beyond the good of my country, best study her interests and the interests of freedom by declining to elevate my name upon the ruin of thousands, and afford our tyrants an apology to draw another chain around unhappy Ireland." " He spoke," says one who witnessed this last flicker of the dying rebellion, " in a subdued and feeling tone, and as he bade them all farewell he appeared deeply affected."

One by one the conspirators melted away into the night, and left Emmet alone with a few of his devoted friends. Every man was now to look to his own safety, but these insisted on sharing their general's peril until he should leave the country by one of those fishing smacks lying off the coast whose owners would only too gladly convey their defeated chief to a place of safety.

Strange seems to have been the infatuation which possessed these doomed men. They drifted from house to house in the vicinity of Dublin without any apparent effort to escape, until Thursday the 28th, when they came very near being captured in the tavern at Bohernbreena. Chilled by the heavy dews, for they had spent the preceding night on the hill-side, they called at William Kearney's house to get refreshment, and, while still at breakfast, Constable Robinson came unsuspiciously into the inn; however, his approach had been seen, and the fugitives were already hidden in a kind of cockloft reached by a narrow staircase. At about eleven o'clock one of the staff, who was looking out of the little skylight, their only window, perceived a party of five hundred men approaching, commanded by Mr. de la Touche. The alarm was immediately given. Kearney, who was a quick-witted fellow, throwing some baskets of turf on the stairway, prepared to receive the militiamen. Robert Shaw, as second officer, demanded to know who was within. The tavern keeper replied, "No one, sir; the house is not large and you can easily see through it." Observing the means of access to the loft, he inquired if there was anyone above stairs. Kearney answered, with great sangfroid, that there was not. "We use the place," said he, "for light lumber; it is not able to bear anything heavy on it." All this time Devlin lay crouching above, his blunderbuss covering the approach to their hiding-place, and had Shaw attempted the ascent, his life would have surely been the forfeit. Not satisfied with the landlord's answer, he put his foot on the first step, when Mrs. Kearney gently detained him, saying, " Oh, sir, if you go up there you will fall through and be killed." Shaw seems not to have been deaf to this appeal, and withdrew.

That evening this little band of brave spirits parted company, to meet no more. Neil O'Dwyer begged his chief to go with him into Wicklow, where he could easily hide until a chance of escape should present itself; but Emmet, although urged by his staff to accept this offer, steadily refused, saying; " No, I would not for any consideration go near Dwyer after our defeat." That night he made his way back to Dublin, having determined to seek one more interview with Sarah Curran before leaving his native land forever. For that interview he threw his life into the balance, and lost it. On reaching the city he again went to Mrs. Palmer's, under the name of Hewitt, from whence he addressed several letters to Miss Curran; but his hopes of gaining speech with her were frustrated by his sudden capture.

On the evening of August 25th, Major Sirr rang the door-bell, and, rushing past Mrs. Palmer's little girl, who answered it, entered the back parlor where Emmet was sitting and placed him under arrest. Then dismissing the mother and child, and having set his orderly to guard the prisoner, he questioned them separately as to their lodger's name and the length of time he had resided with them. Their accounts being materially different from that given by Emmet, he returned to the room where he had left his prisoner, to find him covered with blood from a blow levelled at him by the guard while attempting to escape. Sirr then lost no time in calling an escort from Canal Bridge to conduct Emmet to the castle, where he was identified by one of his old college enemies, the Provost of Trinity. Emmet made one more effort for liberty and life; but Sirr, overtaking him, frustrated his object. When Emmet saw that escape was impossible, he surrendered. Sirr made some sort of apology for the rough treatment given him; but with that sweet temper which never deserted him, the patriot answered that it was " all fair in war."

He was committed to Kilmainham Jail to await his trial, and received better usage than was common toward the political prisoners who were unfortunate enough to come under the care of Dr. Trevor.

Mason, Emmet's cousin, who occupied the next cell to his, and whose chief crime seems to have been his relationship to the unsuccessful conspirator, concocted a plan of escape for Robert; but, unfortunately, George Dunn, the keeper, on whom depended their schemes, was a man whose very name pollutes the pages of history. After receiving the bribes of these helpless men, and having deluded them with the hope of escape, he informed John Dunn, the prison governor, of their intentions, and also handed him a letter to Miss Curran which Emmet had pledged him by all things holy to deliver safely into her own keeping. The encouragement policy was again adopted and Emmet, " all unknowing," carried on constant communications with Mason, which were duly inspected by the prison authorities. Dr. Trevor also stationed a man in the room above the cells occupied by the political prisoners, who, having bored holes through the floor, watched their movements, and overheard their conversations through this modern ear of Dionysus.

Emmet requested Curran to defend

him at his trial, but was refused in rather harsh terms, if we are to judge by the prisoner's gently remonstrant letter in which he tells with directness and simplicity the story of his unhappy love.

On hearing that his note to Sarah was in the hands of the Government, Emmet was desperate. He offered to tell all he knew of the conspiracy, saving the names of the participants, provided only that the letter was suppressed. Again, he promised to offer no defence and call no witness at his trial. Lastly, knowing how anxious his enemies were that he should not speak to the people from the scaffold, he promised to die silently. This last sacrifice propitiated the castle authorities, and the letter, for which poor Sarah Curran would no doubt have given years of her life, was allowed to drift down the tide of forgotten State documents.

Shortly before his trial one of the keepers, coming suddenly in upon him and seeing a peculiar expression on his face, made an apology for intruding. "No," said Emmet; "you see I am innocently employed." Pointing to a fork driven into the table to which he had attached a lock of hair, he added, "This little tress has long been dear to me; I am plaiting it to wear at my trial." It is needless to say the hair was hers for love of whom he had imperilled his life.

So great was his gentleness and so magnetic his personality, that even in these humiliating circumstances he managed to win the affections of the turnkey of his ward and command the esteem of the prison governor.

On Monday, September 19, 1803, Robert Emmet was brought for trial before a special commission, consisting of Lord Norbury, George, and Daley. The court assigned as counsel for him Messrs. Ball, Burrows and McNally— O'Grady and thrice-perjured Plunket acting for the Crown.

Emmet was dressed in black, with the exception of his white shorts and silk stockings—it was afterward discovered that the little braid of Sarah Curran's hair was folded inside his stock. Thus did he march to hear the sentence of death, armed with a conscience void of offence, and comforted only by the memory of his love.

The witnesses for the Crown proved beyond doubt his participation in the rebellion, but, as he had promised, he made no effort at defence. However, when Plunket rose to reply, his counsel pleaded that as there was no testimony called in behalf of the prisoner, there was no occasion for further prosecution. But Plunket would not avail of this permission to throw silence like a cloak over the many-colored vesture of his own politics. This facile gentleman, who but a few years ago had declaimed in flowing phrases, to the advocates of the Union, that he would defend it with the last drop of his blood, and "when he felt the hour of his dissolution approaching" he, like Hannibal, would take his children to the altar and swear them to eternal hostility against the invaders of his country's freedom—now, when the hope of Ireland's emancipation seemed flown forever, stretched the furthest limits of the court to heap vituperative epithets on the head of him who had but embraced the doctrines Plunket had advocated. Silence now fell upon the vast assembly. Every eye turned eagerly toward the jury, who, without leaving the box, rendered the verdict of " Guilty." Then rose such a yell of concentrated fury from the crowd that it shook the judge upon the bench; so terrible that the foreman, turning pale, sought military protection.

Amid the oppressive silence which ensued, Lord Norbury read the death-warrant, ending with the formal question, " What have you to say why sentence of death and execution should not be awarded against you ?" Then, like the lightning from some dark cloud, flashed Emmet's eye, and like an impetuous torrent bearing all before it rolled on the flood of his irresistible eloquence. Then did he vindicate his stainless honor in that oration delivered, "To time and to eternity, and not to man." We have no perfect record of this wonderful defence; but, like the stray diamonds of a broken necklet, here and there his words, garnered in the loving hearts of his countrymen, come flashing out to give us an approximate idea of the perfect beauty of the whole.

It was ten o'clock at night when, through the silent streets of Dublin, passed the military escort, bearing with them a condemned prisoner toward Newgate. Emmet was here delivered over to the tender mercies of Grigg. This worthy emissary of the castle-government placed the unhappy patriot in a condemned cell and loaded his exhausted frame with irons. But not yet was the necessary rest and quiet vouchsafed him. At midnight came a detachment of soldiers with a warrant "to remove the traitor, Robert Emmet, to his old quarters at Kilmainham."

Off again they marched through the starlight and the silence of the sleeping city. It was supposed that the Government had received some intimation of a projected rescue, and that it was on this account that the last hours of the condemned man were so ruthlessly intruded upon.

When the party reached the jail the prisoner's ankles were severely lacerated by the fetters; yet, though weakened by loss of blood, overcome by the fatigues of the previous day and the want of food, his uncomplaining fortitude seems to have touched even the heart of a prison official. With tears in his eyes

George Dunn ordered Emmet's chains removed and refreshment to be provided for him.

As he passed the cell of one of his fellow-conspirators, stepping close to the grating he whispered, "I am to be hanged to-morrow," and then went quietly by, so great was his self-control. He spent the remainder of the night in writing. To his brother, Thomas Addis, he sent a detailed account of the proposed plan of attack and defence. To the two Currans he also wrote letters, and, although addressed to Richard, one of these communications was evidently intended for the perusal of his unhappy ladylove. In it he says: "I intended as much happiness for Sarah as the most ardent love could have given. I never did tell you how much I idolized her;" and again: "My love, Sarah, I did hope to be a prop round which your affections might have clung, and which would never have been shaken; but a rude blast has snapped it, and they have fallen over a grave." Nor did he allow personal considerations to monopolize his attention, even in the face of death. Knowing that all Ireland listened breathless, that she might catch every word dropped by the departing hero, he took occasion to write that noble praise of the governmental clemency which the constant interruptions of the judge had prevented his delivering in court.

The spectacle of such magnanimity shining amidst the gathering shadows of annihilation is as beautiful as it is rare.

The prison minister was with him when McNally arrived, bringing the news of Mrs. Emmet's death. This highminded and true-hearted woman, who, like Rebecca, staked all her hopes upon her youngest son, could not survive his trial. She expired during the night. Emmet, knowing of her illness, and probably alarmed by McNally's face, immediately questioned him about his mother. His counsel then told him of his calamity, as gently as possible. For a few moments he stood silently struggling to suppress his emotion, then saying, " It is better so," turned resignedly away to prepare his soul for eternity. A sincere Christian, Emmet experienced no fear of death; borne up by the consciousness of his own integrity of purpose, and the worthiness of the cause for which he suffered, he completely ignored the disgrace and obloquy attendant on the scaffold. So perfectly had he overcome any feeling of this kind that, a few hours before his young life was quenched forever, he sketched upon the table of his cell a head severed from the trunk and surrounded by all the paraphernalia of an execution. The face, it is said, was an excellent likeness of himself.

At about one o'clock they came to lead him forth; he received the summons with that fortitude which, indeed, never deserted him. "I have," he said, "two requests; the first, that my arms may be left as loose as possible. I make the other, not under any idea that it will be granted, but that it may be held in remembrance that I have made it. It is, that I may be permitted to die in my uniform." The first of these favors was humanely accorded him; the second, as he divined, was refused. He bade good-by with much kindness to those around him, especially to the turnkey who had particularly attended to him. This poor fellow had in those few days learned to love his noble charge, and the tears were streaming down his rugged face. Emmet's hands being tied, leaning over, he gently kissed him on the forehead. Now they passed out into the open street. Along their way men and women stood watching for a last look of him who was to die because he loved his Ireland too well to brook the destruction of her liberties. At the windows of all the houses anxious faces peered out to catch the first sign of his approach.

It was no hollow mourning, such as follows a king when, bereft of crown and sceptre, he is borne in state to rest in the grave of his ancestors. This condemned criminal had placed upon his young brow the better diadem of a people's love, and every Irishman felt the sharp blow that severed him from life as though that life, so precious to them all, were indeed interwoven with their very heartstrings.

Guarded by a strong military escort he passed to the place of execution, and, as the carriage moved on, ever and anon would he nod to some acquaintance in the street or at the windows. Love met him in every eye; blessings followed him from every heart. Thus the cortége bore more resemblance to the obsequies of a hero than the exit of a condemned criminal. At one place on the route they passed a carriage with but a single occupant. As he neared the spot Emmet put his head out of the window and motioned with his poor, bound hand. The young woman in the vehicle stood up a moment to wave her handkerchief, then sinking back she covered her face, overcome with emotion. Emmet continued to gaze after her as long as she remained in sight. This was his last meeting on earth with Sarah Curran; but their separation was not for long. Bowed down by a load of grief, too heavy for her slight frame, she died of a broken heart, in scarcely more than a year— following him she loved so well to that bourn from whence no traveller has returned. The patriot's dauntless courage never faltered. He ascended the scaffold with a firm step, and, turning to those around him, said: "My friends, I die in peace, and with sentiments of universal love and kindness to all men."

"Irish soil drank the blood of her loving son, but it still cries from the ground, pleading for the liberty to secure which he sacrificed his life."

In the deserted churchyard of St. Michins there is a slab on which no name is traced. Beneath this stone rest the ashes of Robert Emmet. How long, oh, Ireland, how long will it remain without an epitaph!

Thus died Ireland's true knight, sinking into the grave clothed in all the bright promise of his youth; never to put on the sad livery of age; never to feel the hopelessness of those who live to see the principles for which they suffered trampled and forgotten by the onward march of new interests and new men. Perhaps Freedom, like some deity of ancient Greece, loved him too well to let the "slurs and contumely of outrageous fortune" dim the bright lustre of his virgin fame. Was it that in every revolution there must be some sacrifice to fill the ravenous jaws of watchful tyranny e'er the new liberated people can march forward to the fruition of their hopes? Or is it that the graves of those who fall, like road-side crosses, point new generations on the road to freedom?

"Man dies, but his memory lives," and the name of Emmet shall ever awaken an answering thrill in Irish breasts as long as the shamrock grows green on the hills of Tara, and as long as the sea moans among the rocks of Connaught.

Man dies, but the principles which animated him are in their very essence immortal; like the phœnix, they sink into their ashes only to rise again, doubly resplendent, upon the wings of hope.

Ireland stands now with outstretched hands eagerly waiting the advent of her freedom. Now has she climbed with tireless feet the rugged path which alone leads to Liberty's demesne. Who, then, shall say that those have failed who, with their very heart's blood, fed the watchfires for her guidance, who deemed it glory to be accounted worthy of such sacrifice? That patriot-blood may be the talisman to break the chains that ever bound her down, the veriest slave, at England's mercy; and now, that in the near future we may see—oh, blessed vision!—a new era dawn upon this beautiful but unhappy land, let us reverently remember those who died martyrs in the effort to serve their countrymen.

"Oh not for idle hatred, not for honor, fame, nor
    self-applause,
  But for the glory of the cause
  You did what will not be forgot."

Varina Anne Davis.

www.ingramcontent.com/pod-product-compliance
Lightning Source LLC
Chambersburg PA
CBHW020257090426
42735CB00009B/1118